W9-BOM-598

THIS BOOK IS LITERALLY JUST PICTURES OF SNOOZY ANIMALS THAT WILL MAKE YOU SLEEP BETTER

Smith Street Books

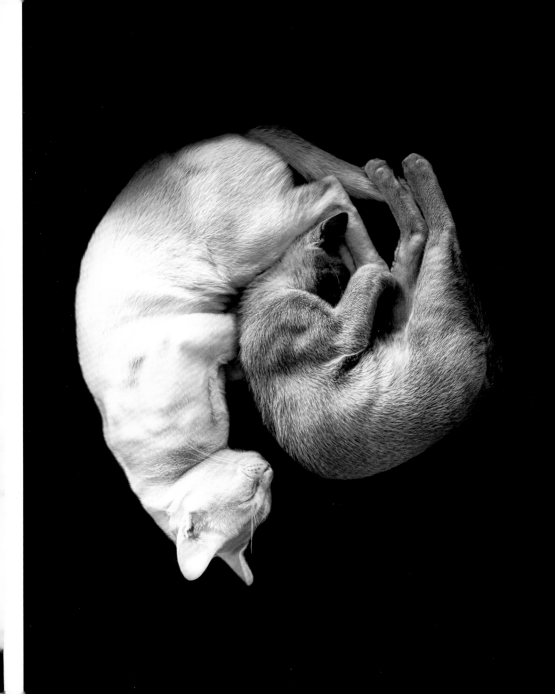

Published in 2020 by Smith Street Books
Melbourne | Australia
smithstreetbooks.com

ISBN: 978-1-92581-138-4

All rights reserved. No part of this book may be reproduced or
transmitted by any person or entity, in any form or means, electronic
or mechanical, including photocopying, recording, scanning or by any
storage and retrieval system, without the prior written permission of
the publishers and copyright holders.

Copyright cover photo © maksymowicz / Adobe Stock Images
Copyright design © Smith Street Books

CIP data is available from the National Library of Australia.

Publisher: Paul McNally
Design and layout: Hannah Koelmeyer
Cover photo: maksymowicz / Adobe Stock Images

Printed & bound in China by C&C Offset Printing Co., Ltd.

Book 113
10 9 8 7 6 5 4 3 2 1